# DARK AND DASTARDLY
# DARTMOOR

## Sally and Chips Barber

*Ghost Shepherd of Dartmoor Prison*

**OBELISK PUBLICATIONS**

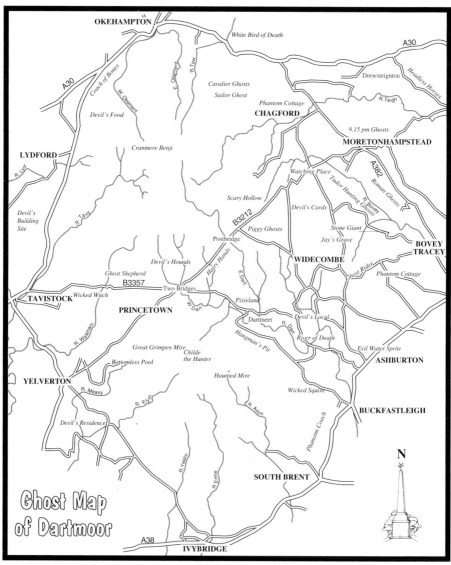

Ghost Map of Dartmoor

We have over 120 Devon titles – for full catalogue, or Dartmoor titles only, please send 1st class stamp to Obelisk Publications at 2 Church Hill, Pinhoe, Exeter, EX4 9ER or telephone (01392) 468556.

All drawings by Jane Reynolds, All photos by or belonging to Chips Barber,
Map of Dartmoor redrawn from an out-of-copyright source by Sally Barber

*First published in 1988 (0 946651 26 4) Reprinted in 1990 and 1992.*
*Revised edition printed in 1994 (0 946651 98 1) Reprinted in 1995*
*by Obelisk Publications, 2 Church Hill, Pinhoe, Exeter, Devon*
*Designed by Chips and Sally Barber/Typeset by Sally Barber*
*Printed in Great Britain by The Devonshire Press Limited, Torquay, Devon*

# Introduction

If you stand alone on the top of a Dartmoor tor, particularly on a dreary, misty day, and scan the far horizons you will begin to appreciate that this is a unique environment. Despite a first impression of being a barren wasteland, here is an ancient landscape that has witnessed many events both mundane and extraordinary. It is therefore steeped in a wealth of folklore, legends and ghost stories, some based on fact, others passed by word of mouth by people who have lived and worked here for generations.

Having read almost every book that has ever been written about Dartmoor (and published a few ourselves!) we've found that, although most books retell the same stories, the details often differ. We decided to write this little book as a compilation of the genuinely bizarre or ghostly stories that we've come across. It is intended to both entertain and inform you about some of the many strange tales Dartmoor has thrown up through the murky mists of time. If you believed every tale you would probably never set foot in the place again because, as will be revealed, Dartmoor must have more ghosts than people living on it. If you throw in the Devil, headless horses, talking rivers, and pigs that wear wigs, phantom cottages, and many more weird and wonderful tales, you have the makings of a truly sinister and supernatural place!

## When is a Ghost not a Ghost?

The solution to this riddle can be answered quite simply if the scene is a Dartmoor bog in the late evening or twilight. If you see a pale bluish flame flickering evanescently then this is (probably) no spirit intent on luring you to a marshy demise. "Ignis fatuus", or as we would call it "will-o'-the-wisp", is a natural phenomenon that occasionally appears over marshes. This strange natural occurrence is also called "jack-o'lantern" and, seen from a distance, it is easy to see how it might perpetrate strange stories.

## Well I Be Boggered!

We couldn't resist the temptation to include the following story, a favourite tale told by a former senior Dartmoor National Park Officer, which centres on the infamous depths of a Dartmoor mire.

A young man was wending his way home, on foot, across the moor when he came across a valley bog with very treacherous parts – the locals call them "Feather Beds" or "Quakers". The young moor man espied a rather fine top hat resting delicately on the mire and, unable to resist the temptation, he picked it up – only to find that beneath it was a man's head. The immersed gentleman smiled, and introduced himself very politely, and the moor man immediately offered to assist him out of his obvious predicament. His offer of help was accepted – but only on condition that the young man also rescued the horse on which he was seated!

## The Great Grimpen Mire

Whilst we are on the subject of bogs, the famous Great Grimpen Mire was based on Foxtor Mires when Sir Arthur Conan Doyle used his fertile imagination to turn a local legend into a powerful drama. His Dartmoor-based story, *The Hound of the Baskervilles*,

*The Whiteworks and Foxtor Mires*

has been dramatized on numerous occasions, several versions for both television and film having been filmed on the moor.

Conan Doyle regularly used to visit friends who lived near Ipplepen in Devon. On one of his outings he visited the Royal Duchy Hotel at Princetown (which at one time became the prison officers' mess and is now a visitors' centre) where

he heard the story of a notorious character called Squire Cabell. This evil person, who died in 1677, scared the local populace so much, even in death, that his coffin was secured by an enormous slab to make sure he didn't get out again! His coffin was then entombed within a small building at Buckfastleigh.

Cabell had been a huntsman who, according to legends, sold his soul to the Devil. It is rumoured that phantom black hounds came to howl around his burial chamber and presumably all the precautions against him came to naught as stories are told of his ghostly hunt being heard in full cry.

This made excellent literary fodder for turning into a first rate meal of a story although, as in all good stories, the names of actual people and places have been changed to protect

Dark and Dastardly Dartmoor

*Buckfastleigh Church as it was before being severely damaged by fire*

the innocent. Conan Doyle demonstrated his tongue-in-cheek sense of humour, when choosing a suitably grand and impressive name for the ill-fated family, by using the name of the man who acted as his pony trap driver to Princetown!

## Childe the Hunter

Some Dartmoor legends are so well known that they become tedious in the retelling and this traditional tale of sheer stupidity and out and out greed is one of them.

However, for those who don't know the tale, Childe was a bachelor, the last of a long family line of well-to-do country folk. As he had no heirs, he inserted into his will a clause that stated whichever church should bury him would then possess all his lands.

Then, duly endowed with death assurance, Childe went out onto the moor, in the depths of a snowy winter, to

Dark and Dastardly Dartmoor

5

*Childe's Tomb*

hunt. Somehow he became separated from the hunting party and became hopelessly lost on the southern moor about four miles to the south of Princetown. The flurry of snow, which had drifted large flakes down on to the moor all day, turned into a full scale blizzard. At this point Childe made a fatal mistake, his judgement obviously impaired by the numbing cold. He cut off his lifeline, his horse, by killing and disembowelling it, then climbed inside its carcass for shelter and warmth. His final act was to leave a message in blood (there was probably a great deal of it around from his dead horse!) written in the snow, reiterating his wishes.

For days afterwards it snowed and his frozen corpse lay out on the wasteland until a traveller chanced upon it. Presumably his message was still legible as this gentleman, who was bound north-westwards, spread the news of Childe's death and last request. As soon as the Friars at Tavistock and the Monks of Childe's native Plymstock got to hear the news, the race was on to fulfil the demands of Childe's will. The Friars of Tavistock reached the body first and made haste back to their town, but the Monks lay in wait at the bridge where they expected the Friars to cross the River Tavy. However the Friars got wind of the Monks' plan and cleverly erected their own pontoon over the River, at a spot today known as Guile Bridge. They then managed to intern the body safely and claim their entitlement. All in all the whole saga sounds like a medieval version of *Jeux Sans Frontières*.

## Bowerman's Nose

On the northern slopes of Hayne Down, about a mile from Hound Tor, is a strange rock idol called Bowerman's Nose, an enormous human-like shaped granite stack. It is a natural formation but at one time it was believed to be man made or, more accurately, magically formed for, according to ancient tradition, this pile of rock was actually a brave, but foolish giant called Bowerman.

Bowerman was another hunter

who scoured the moors with his powerful pack of ferocious hounds. Although a strong man he was a genial, cheerful chap and was much loved by the moorland community. However, in the days when he lived the local witch population was large and very active in their dark pursuits.

One day a fateful confrontation occurred between the witches and Bowerman. Hot in pursuit of his quarry, Bowerman drove his pack through a coven of witches who were so outraged at the disruption he caused that they decided to wreak their revenge.

Even Bowerman, so mighty and powerful, did not have the wit, guile or strength to avoid the ambush that the wicked witches set to ensnare him. One of the old hags turned herself into a hare and set off across the moors. She went over hill and dale pursued by the rapidly tiring hounds and hunter until, just as Bowerman thought that he had cornered the hare, he rode headlong into a trap. With venomous intent the witches heaped a combined spell onto him turning both him and his pack to stone. The great rock of Bowerman's Nose is said to be the giant himself, and the boulders strewn across the hillside are his hounds – all petrified for eternity.

## The Hounds of the Devil

Now on to the most famous hunter of all – the Devil! Not for him is the mundane quarry of an ordinary fox or deer; he hunts for the souls of unbaptised babies and if anyone gazes on him or on his pack of spectral hounds they will meet with certain death within a year. It is easy to identify this particular hunting pack as it usually sets off from Wistman's Wood, a half mile north of Two Bridges, at Midnight. The Devil himself rides a headless black horse and the black hounds, known as the Wisht Hounds, with scorching red eyes, do his bidding. It is not uncommon to hear their baying, sometimes quite close by, as they invisibly range across the moor. They chase their victims towards the Dewerstone, driving them over the precipice of this near vertical rock face that is high above the River Plym. Some people say this is where the Devil lives on Dartmoor, at a quiet, detached rocky crag called the Dewerstone, "Dewer" being another name for the Devil.

## When the Devil holds the trump card . . .

Apart from being a keen huntsman, the Devil is also happy to participate in a spot of money lending – but the interest rates are astronomical! Jan Reynolds, a tin miner of bad character, paid the price of selling his soul to the Devil, one night on 21 October 1638.

The Devil, on his way to collect his dues, called at The Tavistock Inn at Poundsgate to quaff some ale and get directions for Widecombe.

WIDECOMBE VILLAGE.

He downed the ale, which sizzled and steamed as it washed down his throat, and paid the landlady with a gold coin. The landlady's glee at the visitor's generosity diminished rather, after he had left, when it turned into a leaf and withered away – confirming that money doesn't grow on trees!

Meanwhile, back at Widecombe-in-the-Moor, in the Church of St Pancras, the unsuspecting Jan Reynolds snoozed as the sermon wore on. In his hand he clutched a pack of cards. Suddenly the Devil turned on a spectacular natural firework display, a thunderstorm of high drama with exploding claps of thunder and enormous bolts of lightning flashing across the sky. Tethering his horse to one of the pinnacles, he burst into the church, seized Jan Reynolds and threw him over his horse. He rode northwards climbing ever higher into the sky. Not far from the Warren House Inn, four of Jan's cards fell to the ground and formed the small fields known as The Devil's Playing Cards, the shapes of each being recognizable as a different suit of cards.

During the storm that night when the church at Widecombe was struck, four people were killed and many more badly injured by falling masonry. The story of this true disaster is told in detail on the walls of the church.

## Brentor—Saint Michael of the Rock

Having been deemed responsible for the near destruction of one church, the Devil has also been blamed for the positioning of the Church of St Michael of the Rock on the volcanic, triangular hill of Brentor. It can be seen from so many places on Dartmoor, the Plymouth area and East Cornwall, that it has to be one of the most distinctive landmarks in South West England. (This high hill has acquired a reputation as a spot visited frequently by UFO's – see *Tales of the Unexplained in Devon*.)

It was the Rev. Sabine Baring-Gould who apportioned the blame to the Devil for its location, in a story he wrote in 1884. It seems that whilst the church was being built the Devil kept stealing all the foundation stones. However, an Archangel took a dim view of this and hid behind Cox Tor, a mass of rocks five miles to the south east. When the Devil turned up to vandalize the builders' efforts, the Archangel threw a massive rock at him. As you might imagine, when a hefty rock tossed over this long distance, hit him between the horns, it gave him an almighty headache. He therefore gave up and the edifice was completed.

Dark and Dastardly Dartmoor

As with all stories of this type there are variations. Legend has it that it was built as a thanksgiving by a sailor who survived a terrible storm, on the first land spotted on reaching safety. However, the location of Brentor makes this a most unlikely possibility!

## Branscombe's Loaf and Cheese

There is a small granite-capped hill, high on Sourton Common and close to Meldon Reservoir, called Branscombe's Loaf. By chance, or a 'slice' of good luck, it has a lovely little story to explain its origin.

In the late thirteenth century Walter Bronescombe or Branscombe was Bishop of Exeter. His diocese stretched across the length and breadth of Devon and Cornwall and, from time to time, he had to travel around the area.

Now, on one particular occasion, whilst accompanied by his chaplain, he strayed from the King Way, the original road from Okehampton to Tavistock, and became lost in the mist. As the time passed by and the mist persisted, the Bishop and his chaplain developed hunger pangs and, as one is wont to say in these circumstances, declared they "would give anything for a bite to eat". Miraculously, to their profound relief, a stranger materialized out of the mist and approached them. The old man, with a skeletal face and frame, produced some bread and cheese. The Bishop was just about to accept this kind offering when the chaplain let out a warning yell. He had spotted that the moor man's foot was cloven, absolute proof that it was the Evil One, Himself, confronting them. The uneaten bread and cheese dropped to the ground and immediately turned into the rocks of that name today.

The mist duly lifted and the Bishop and his chaplain went on their way none the worse for wear, still with rumbling tummies, but infinitely grateful that they hadn't been obliged to pay the ultimate price for the devilish waiter service.

## Cutty Dyer

The ancient stannary and borderland town of Ashburton possesses its own evil little sprite who appears in the shape of Cutty Dyer. He is easy to find as he lives near King's Bridge in the centre of the town. For many generations a visit by him was threatened to naughty children who didn't mend their ways. But misbehaving children were not his sole clients – he was particularly active against those folk who drank too much. He would eagerly waylay anyone in a state of alcoholic stupor as they staggered home. At best they could expect to be thrown into the River Ashburn but at worst this evil little sprite would cut their throats, drink their blood and then throw them into the river!

In the Middle Ages an image or statue of St Christopher, patron saint of travellers, stood beside the river to help travellers when the Ashburn was in flood. Possibly a drunken

reveller destroyed it, which turned the image into this large, red-eyed water sprite – 'Cutty' being a derivative of St Christopher and a 'Dyer' is defined as a scoundrel of the deepest dye – so beware!

## Jan Coo

The Ashburn is not the only Dartmoor river with a penchant for taking human life. The River Dart, which starts as two distinct flows, the East Dart and the West Dart, and then unites at Dartmeet to form the Dart, has acquired a cruel reputation. It even has a rhyming couplet (obviously founded on 'Dart' rhyming rather neatly with 'heart') based on the old superstitious belief that the river 'calls' for a life at least once a year.

The Dart flows with great power beneath towering hills before leaving Dartmoor at Buckfast, and when it's considered just how many people use the river for recreational purposes, it is statistically likely that the river's reputation will live on.

Someone who was convinced the river was calling him was a young orphan lad called Jan Coo who lived at Rowbrook, just below Dartmeet.

One night the boy heard a voice calling his name from the direction of the Dart. Although other workers on the farm could also hear the voice, Jan was convinced it was his name being called. This happened every evening until his curiosity got the better of him. Now, we expect you're thinking the same as us, that with a name like Jan Coo there is a high possibility that local pigeons or cuckoos might well have innocently been calling out 'Coo Coo'. But, so the story goes, young Jan ran off towards the river, and was never seen again – but neither was the eerie voice ever heard again!

## Crazywell Pool

Also renowned for calling out names is Crazywell Pool, situated between Sheepstor and Princetown, endowed with an extremely apt name for a place associated with some strange and bizarre tales.

Crazywell Pool is in the parish of Walkhampton but is actually quite a distance from that village. The locals would always be careful to avoid walking within earshot of the pool as it is said that the name of the next person to die in the parish of Walkhampton is called out by the pool at dusk. Alternatively, a quick visit to the pool at midnight on Midsummer's Day Eve and you would see the face of the next person to die, reflected in the pond. We should imagine that to test this one out is a little chancy as the odds must be that you will see your own reflection!

Some young lads who had sat in a local inn and scoffed at the tale decided to disprove it, with tragic results. They rode their motorcycles up the rough track that rises up from Burrator Reservoir and passes close to the pool. What happened that night will remain a mystery as they were both killed riding home.

It is not a natural lake but an old tin mine, which has filled up with water, and is reputed to be bottomless. This inaccurate theory is based on the story that at one time all the bell ropes of Walkhampton Church were tied together and still failed to reach the bottom. We have been unable to discover if the bells were left on the end of the ropes to weigh them down but as the current consensus measures the pool at a mere 15 feet deep, it seems likely that the ropes were quietly folding up on the bottom!

## Cranmere Benji

Whilst we're on a watery theme, we should take a look at Cranmere Pool, hardly worthy of such a title as, even after heavy rain, it is little more than an overgrown puddle! It was once regarded as the most remote spot on the Moors. Set high on a tableland of morass and mire, it remains a wild location today, although it is just about possible to drive a robust car within a mile of it as the looping, but gradually deteriorating, Artillery Road almost encompasses it.

To stand at Cranmere Pool, even today, is to be at a desolate spot where the wind whistles incessantly and little sign of life will be seen. With all its natural disadvantages this spot became the location of the first 'letterbox' on Dartmoor. In 1854 James Perrot, the celebrated Chagford guide, left a bottle here so that the rare few visitors, each season, could leave their calling cards for others to peruse and act upon. Later postcards were left, the numbers of visitors recorded in the Visitors' book growing greatly as the years passed. Perrot would probably turn in his grave if he knew how his solitary 'box' has become just one of literally thousands hidden on the moor.

One character who knew Cranmere, even before Perrot, was a gentleman from Okehampton called Benjamin Geyer. He was a trader who ran into hard times when several ships laden with his goods were captured by Turkish pirates. Left in a desperate plight he hit on a salvage plan to protect his lifestyle. Without permission he 'borrowed' or appropriated some funds, maintained by public subscription and administered by himself as Mayor of Okehampton. Racked with guilt over his crime, he died in so troubled a state of mind that his spirit would not rest. Each night he could be heard weeping and wailing and gnashing his teeth in Okehampton. As the residents of the town got very upset by the nocturnal noises, even though they were harmless, they called in priests to rid them of their vociferous ghost. They turned him into a black colt and a rider jumped onto his back and rode him at a mighty pace up on to the moor and six miles south to Cranmere Pool. As he approached the pool, the rider jumped off allowing the black colt to disappear, in spectacular fashion, beneath the waves never to be heard sobbing again. Until of course he appears in another version of the story ...

Benjamin Gayer or Gear (also more familiarly Bingie, Binjy or Benjie), Mayor of Okehampton on five occasions, was hanged after being convicted of sheep stealing. His soul was condemned to empty Cranmere Pool with a sieve. However, being a resourceful old soul, and well versed in sheep stealing, he killed another sheep and lined the sieve with the sheepskin. He then easily emptied the pool, so successfully in fact that the waters of the pool cascaded down onto Okehampton, flooding the town.

For this atrocious act he was further sentenced to spin the sand in the bed of the now dry Cranmere Pool, into ropes. This task still employs him as he moans about it on stormy nights – growling and wailing in protest.

## Widecombe-in-the-Moor

We've already seen what the Devil did to Widecombe Church but this small moorland village, made world famous by a folk song about its Fair, has also been troubled by other ghosts.

The Old Inn is haunted by a ghost called "Harry" who occasionally in mid afternoon, walks from the kitchen into a room that has no exit, only solid stone walls, and disappears. He has been seen many times but, unlike the standard see-through, almost wimpish apparition, Harry has a very solid, real look about him. He doesn't scare people because he is so lifelike.

Dark and Dastardly Dartmoor

Within the same inn the sounds of a sobbing child have been heard, in the past, in an upstairs bedroom. She cries for endless hours but when the door is opened the tears subside and there is nobody there!

The Rev. Sabine Baring Gould unearthed many folk songs and ballads on his tours of the West Country but the one about Widecombe Fair is known by most people. In the words of the song it tells us that "when the wind whistles cold on the moor of a night, ... Tom Pearce's old grey mare doth appear ghostly white". If ever an animal had better cause

to reappear as a ghost than this poor creature, then it would be hard to find. Just imagine the scene when seven hulking great country boys living in a band of countryside almost twenty long moorland miles to the north of Widecombe all decided to visit Widecombe Fair. But, as this is long before the age of motor cars or buses, they grab the poor old grey mare, scramble aboard and expect her to carry them to Widecombe so they might drink themselves into a stupor.

Quite clearly the poor old horse couldn't take the strain, collapsed and died. Now, from time to time, the rattlings of her bones are heard in the vicinity of Widecombe. The worthless characters who caused her premature demise with their drunken frolicking have all been named in the song, but the poor old grey mare remains anonymous.

## A Fair Way to Go?

In the early nineteenth century fairs, which were mainly agricultural meets, were important features on the moor man's calendar. Brent Fair was an event not to be missed.

The farmer who lived at Round Hill, on the road from Two Bridges to Princetown, was determined to have a good day out and do a bit of business as well!

Some versions of this sorry tale suggest he sold his old horse to the gypsies for a song,

Dark and Dastardly Dartmoor

got completely drunk and then bought back the same horse for a much higher amount – other versions just say he was cheated on a deal. Either way, he was obviously very unhappy with the outcome.

Meanwhile, waiting back at home, his wife was relieved to hear the unmistakable sounds of his horse plodding into the stable. She waited a few minutes and then, as he did not appear, she lit a lantern and went out to see what was wrong. Outside there was no sign of life, no horse and no husband. The bewildered lady had to wait until the following day to hear the terrible news that he had hanged himself on the way home.

At a point on the road from Holne to Hexworthy, about four miles short of home, he had hanged himself on a tree near Combestone Tor. The place, after that, was always referred to as Hangman's Pit.

## A Phantom Pig Perambulation

Dartmoor is noted for its sheep, cattle and ponies, which are a common sight, wandering freely over the moors. More worthy of a second glance, though, would be the sight of an old sow and her litter of hungry little piglets trotting across the moor.

When the moors are misty and the day is decidedly dull and dreary you might just see such a scene. These may be no ordinary little porky creatures, however, for there is a phantom family, destined to travel the same route from Merripit Hill (the high hill on the Moretonhampstead side of Postbridge) to a venue in the central depression of Dartmoor called Cator Gate. Their journey of a few miles is undertaken, usually on misty days, because they are hungry and have heard of the body of a dead horse at Cator. With great enthusiasm and anticipation they descend to Cator only to find that the horse has already been eaten.

A pathetic scene follows as the little piglets wail and squeal 'Skin and Bones, Skin and Bones' as they disconsolately start their return journey to Merripit Hill. As they trot downheartedly along they become increasingly hungry. Their plight is so acute that they end up emaciated and the cycle of hope and despair is re-enacted once more.

## Judge Jeffreys—The Big Black Phantom Pig

But not all ghostly pigs deserve quite so much sympathy! George Jeffreys, the First Baron Jeffreys, was the English judge who became notorious for his harsh sentencing at the Bloody Assizes after the Monmouth Rebellion in 1685. His severe sentencing for even minor indiscretions earned him a black reputation.

In his travels as a judge on the Western Circuit he held court in many Devonshire towns and legend suggests he was at his judicial best (or worst) at Lydford. Although solid 'evidence' of his ever having been to Lydford is scarce, he must have had a great impact on the area as, so the story goes, he haunts the ancient borough in the guise of a big black pig!

It is not clear how often this phantom porker has been seen or why indeed it should automatically be assumed it was the dreadful judge himself as, so the story goes (again) he is also supposed to haunt a room in a hotel in Exeter – but at least here he is in more recognizable human form!

Whether or not it is he, and whether or not he haunts, you will have to judge for yourself!

## The White Bird of Oxenham

South Zeal is a small village located on the northern side of Dartmoor. It lies between the A30 and the towering Cosdon or Cawsand Hill and is the scene of one of Dartmoor's strangest sequences of events. There is a lovely old stone pub called The Oxenham Arms, which derived its name from a local family whose history dated back to Elizabeth I. Oxenham Manor, their family home, is about one mile to the north east of South Zeal, as close to the boundary of the Dartmoor National Park as you could get.

Dark and Dastardly Dartmoor

The Oxenham family were haunted by the apparition of a white-breasted bird and for a member to see it virtually sealed their fate and death followed almost immediately. Admittedly some of the Oxenhams who died were already on their death beds when the white bird fluttered over them, but there were also sightings by healthy members who met with untimely deaths. 'Lady' Margaret Oxenham had a visitation on the eve of her wedding. Her father saw it fluttering over her head but said nothing. Perhaps if he had she might have been warned to watch out for on the following day, at her wedding, a jealous lover rushed into South Tawton Church and plunged a knife into Margaret's back, then pulled it out to kill himself.

It should be pointed out that it was not just the disordered imagination of a dying person who saw the bird each time as many respectable witnesses, in full control of their faculties, would all swear to having seen the bird. William Oxenham, from the eighteenth century, was feeling slightly off colour when the bird was sighted over him. He boldly proclaimed that he might be sick but he certainly wasn't **that** sick. Within three days he was dead and buried!

The white bird followed the family around until the last of the Oxenham line passed away in Canada this century. Unfortunately no-one noticed whether the bird hopped over the Atlantic and decided to stay in Canada or whether in fact it never saw off its last victim. What is known though is his father's death, in Exeter early this century, certainly was preceded by a visit from a white bird. There are of course many pigeons around the city centre, but even if one had accidentally found its way into the death chamber – it certainly is an odd coincidence!

## Lady Howard

There is no telling what sort of sentence Judge Jeffreys may have inflicted on Lady Howard who, according to the folklore story, supposedly murdered her four husbands. This story has developed as a result of mistaken identity as the deeds of one Lady Frances Howard have been attributed to another Lady Mary Howard. Perhaps this is why her ghost is such a bizarre manifestation. If you do see her then take some consolation in the fact that her only real crime was to cut off her children's inheritance.

Nevertheless, she is doomed to a never-ending chore. She has to visit Okehampton

Castle every night to pluck a single blade of grass. The castle was part of the Fitzford Estates and she was the granddaughter of Sir John Fitz of Fitzford near Tavistock. It is her ghoulish means of transport to the castle and the nature of the journey that is so remarkable, even for a legend.

Lady Howard becomes a big black dog. She runs beside a coach or carriage, which is constructed from the bones of the four husbands she is alleged to have murdered. If you throw in four headless horses and a headless coachman you are left with quite a bizarre spectacle.

The whole entourage has to travel from Fitzford near Tavistock to Okehampton and back. Weird as her mode of transport may be, she is indeed very fortunate that she doesn't have to rely on public transport on this route! She doesn't use the A386 because it didn't exist in the days when she began her sorties into the night. Instead she uses the original route, which scales the heights of the moor, and one can only imagine the awful weather she must encounter at times when she embarks on her nightly quest. Occasionally she has been spotted just off the route. At Bridestowe she has been seen at The Royal Oak and also at the Ghost Tree, which after all, has to be the ideal spot for a ghost dog!

## His Master's Vengeance

Another black dog is to be found on the road from Princetown to Plymouth. Local legend says that he was the pet of a traveller murdered many years ago, and he travels the lonely road looking for the murderer of his master so he might take his revenge. Unfortunately he has been known to make mistakes ... In the last century a visitor was walking along in winter when he was joined by the companionable animal. Fond of dogs he tried to pat its head but was suitably alarmed when his hand passed right through it. Suddenly, a flash of lightning struck him and he wasn't found until the next day – still unconscious – but obviously lucky to be alive!

## The Dog-goned Ponsworthy Pig

Yet another black dog was found wandering near Ponsworthy by a local chap who just happened to be on the way back from the pub at Hexworthy. He tied his scarf around the dog's neck and led him home, locking him in his stable for the night. The following morning when he invited his neighbours to inspect his captive, he was embarrassed to find his scarf tied around the neck of a large black pig! We rather think that the spirit in this story owes more to the Forest Inn at Hexworthy than to the spirit world!

## Squire Fulford

Lady Howard's coach is not the only one on Dartmoor to be pulled by headless horses. There is a haunted house on the eastern side of Dartmoor called Great Fulford (see *Haunted Happenings in Devon*). One of the old Squire Fulford's coaches has occasionally been seen near Dunsford, driven along the lanes by the old cavalier gentleman himself. This phantom coach is pulled by four headless horses but sadly history doesn't tell us the reason for the Squire's outings.

## More Headless Horses

Several decades ago a young man proudly took his friends in his new car off on a jaunt across the moors. As they reached high ground they became enveloped by a thick mist and soon mistook the line of the road and drifted on to open moorland. They immediately realized their mistake but the mist was so dense they could not see the road at all.

As in all good ghost stories, instead of staying in the safety of the car, they got out to look for the road. Suddenly, to their great astonishment, they heard the sound of thundering hooves quickly bearing down on them. As they gazed into the mist they were transfixed by the ghostly sight of several headless horses all mounted by headless riders, menacingly encircling them. Fearing for their lives they cranked the engine (we said it was a few years ago!), dropping the starting handle in the panic. They drove frantically away, fortunately regaining the road after a bit of bumping and skidding.

A day or so later, when the conditions were a little better, the young man, decided to go back for his starting handle (now be honest – would you have gone within 10 miles of the place?) He located the spot and retrieved the lost tool. Embedded in the ground he saw not only the footprints of himself and his friends, plus the tyre marks of his car, but also the hoof prints of galloping and stomping horses. But they did not lead away from or up to the spot!

A similar event occurred when the Chagford Home Guard were on duty at Gidleigh, one night in 1943. On a clear bright, moonlit night the sound of galloping hooves raced up to and past them but no pony was to be seen.

## The Ghost Tor Rider

Between Powder Mills and Two Bridges the B3212 passes below an eminent pile of rocks called Crockern Tor. This point is close to the centre of Dartmoor and was used from 1305 to 1749 for open air meetings of the Tinners' or Stannary Parliament (Stannum is Latin for tin). The tor was chosen because it was about an equal distance for the twenty-four representatives who were sent from each of the four Stannary towns situated in each corner or 'quarter' of the moor. They might well have had an uninvited member joining

them at their twice-yearly meetings for 'Old Crockern' favoured dark nights for his adventures · across Dartmoor. This mysterious horseman had a skeleton steed and was a truly frightening sight to behold.

It is believed that he may well have been associated with the Wisht Hounds as their 'kennel' in Wistman's Wood lies just over the hill from Crockern Tor. Nobody knows who this mysterious rider is or why he haunts this tor and surrounding moor.

## Another Phantom Rider

The road from Haytor towards Widecombe is much used by visitors to eastern Dartmoor. There is a stretch of it which curves and twists below Rippon Tor and leads, in a short while, to the crossroads at Hemsworthy Gate. A phantom rider has been known to speed along here,

from time to time, and can be identified by his distinctive silver hair and an old fashioned military style mackintosh. There is not a lot of point in following him as you can be sure that by the time Hemsworthy Gate is reached he will dissolve into thin air!

Other reports have indicated that a phantom coach (of the coach and horses variety) also clatters along this stretch.

## The A38 Ghosts

The A38 Exeter to Plymouth road skirts the southern edge of Dartmoor and passes by old Dartmoor towns and villages such as Ashburton, Buckfastleigh, South Brent and Ivybridge. Today's road is a fast highway, a great motorized conveyor belt, which happens to be haunted by a hitchhiking ghost (see *Haunted Happenings in Devon* for the full story). However, in the past the route between Devon's premier settlements was a much quieter coaching route, except of course when the midnight coach thundered through the night during the 1830s and 40s. This coach has travelled along the old road at various times since then but, although the unmistakable sounds of horses' hooves and rattling wheels can be clearly heard, the coach is never seen – perhaps this is why the phantom hitchhiker never uses it!

## The Hairy Hands

Of the many stories that abound on Dartmoor, this is the one of which most people  have heard. Possibly this is because most people, at some time, have travelled the stretch of road and anyone who knows the tale will make quite sure that their fellow travellers also know the story!

Shortly after 1910 a series of strange incidents occurred along the B3212 road between Postbridge and Two Bridges or, to put it another way, between the East and West Dart Rivers. Most of the incidents occurred near a farm called Archerton near Postbridge. Cyclists felt their handlebars wrenched out of their hands, turning them into the ditch and even pony traps were put out of control and ended up in the ditch beside the road. Later cars and motor coaches suffered similar fates, sometimes with fatal results. A local man, Dr Helby, from Princetown, rode his motorbike and sidecar, which inexplicably went out of control. Two children, passengers in the sidecar, were thrown out and survived but the doctor was killed. Shortly afterwards an Army officer was injured on his motorcycle along this stretch but survived to reveal that a pair of large, muscular hairy hands closed over his own and forced him off the road.

This revelation led to sensational front page headlines. The *Daily Mail* sent reporters to investigate the story and their reports resulted in a full scale enquiry by the various road authorities into the state of the road. It was always possible that an adverse camber could have caused problems, and repairs were carried out to the road surface.

But that wouldn't explain why, one night in the mid 1920s, a lady in a caravan parked on this stretch of the road, saw a large hairy hand clawing its way up the outside of the window. In sheer panic she made a sign of the cross and the Hairy Hand disappeared never

to be seen by her again! But then again, if she had any sense, she wouldn't have hung around long enough for it to reappear!

Between 1910 and 1930 there was a spate of serious incidents but since those times the strange occurrences, which have undoubtedly happened along that road, have not been as dramatic. There was at least one fatal accident involving an overturned car but as the young occupant was found dead at the scene, we will never know whether the Hairy Hands played a murderous role or whether indeed it was simply an accident. Nevertheless, many folk will always feel a sense of unease, particularly between the Cherry Brook bridge and Postbridge and keep a wary eye out for any hairy intruders,

It is not only this stretch of the B3212 that is haunted because just over a mile to the north east of The Warren House Inn is a spot where the road roller coasters down into a hollow before rising again. This tiny stream, at the head of Green Combe, is the East Bovey River. Whether or not it is the sudden sharp drop into this deep hollow that causes it is not clear, but several people (and dogs) have experienced sudden cold and been overcome with great fear at this spot. Cyclists have complained that they have felt their bicycles enduring such great stresses that they felt they were about to fall apart, only to be perfectly all right again on the ascending opposite side of the depression.

## The Watching Place

About four miles from Moretonhampstead, on the B3212 road over Dartmoor, is a mysterious and sinister spot called the Watching Place. It is located where the road is met by the B3344, which wends its way from the Manaton direction. Its name appears on the sign post but its origin is worthy of some consideration.

It is believed that the local Lord of the Manor once possessed the right to have a gallows on the edge of his lands.

Dark and Dastardly Dartmoor

This particular gallows at the Watching Place was far from redundant with a large proportion of its customers being drawn from the highwaymen trade, some of these footpads being left to dangle long after their death as an example to any others contemplating similar exploits. The Watching Place was thus where relatives or friends had to wait and watch before being allowed to remove their dead.

Alternatively, it has been suggested that the Watching Place is where the highwaymen actually watched out for their intended victims. Whoever it was who did the watching, it has been known for animals, ridden, lead or driven to react strongly to passing this point, experiencing a feeling perhaps of being watched?

## The Warren House

The Warren House Inn is an isolated inn on the Moreton to Postbridge road but a few centuries ago when the original inn stood on the opposite side of the road to the present one, the innkeeper and his family would have lead an extremely isolated

existence. The bulk of their custom would have come from the tin miners who worked the many mines in the vicinity of the inn.

An amusing story that has been passed around for many years, tells of how, at the end of a spell of wintry weather, when the moors had been covered in snow for weeks, a visitor called at the inn in search of overnight accommodation. He was shown to his room in which was a large chest. The visitor stared at it for ages wondering what treasures it might contain until, eventually his curiosity got the better of him. As he lifted the heavy lid he had the shock of his life for inside was a corpse with an extremely white, ghostly face. Thinking he had uncovered a murder victim he ran downstairs screaming. Almost nonchalantly the landlord said, 'Don't worry, tiz only feyther'. 'Father' had died a few weeks earlier and his corpse had been salted down to preserve it until the weather relented and it could be carried for burial at the parish church many miles away across the moor.

There is however another story, which might well be construed as murder. Two men in the inn had an argument over their drinks and one threatened the other. A few nights later, unseen by his victim, he drew a 'magic circle' in chalk around the man's feet. Sure enough, within a short time, his opponent took ill and passed away!

## Ephraim's Pinch

Soussons is a massive coniferous forest that can be seen sprawling over the low hills to the south of the B3212 near the Warren House Inn. Trees cover most of the small hill called Ephraim's Pinch on the south side of this forest. The name is derived from an old story about a young man who had to show his would-be father-in-law that he had sufficient strength and fortitude to be worthy as a suitor to the farmer's daughter.

The task was set. Ephraim had to carry a bag of wheat six miles from Widecombe to Runnage, a farm in the vicinity of Soussons, have it ground and then carry it back without once putting it down for a rest. Ephraim was so determined not to fail that he strained himself badly and died from his injuries. The little hill where he collapsed is thus named in honour of his gallant, or foolish attempt, to win his loved one.

## Princetown's Phantoms

To most people 'Dartmoor' is the prison and it is this grim edifice that springs to mind whenever its name is mentioned. Initially this place of confinement was set up as a Prisoner of War Depot to accommodate thousands of French prisoners and later, in 1812, many Americans. In 1850 it became a convict prison and throughout its years many men have died there.

David Davies was sent there in 1879 and, over two terms of almost consecutive imprisonment, spent a total of 50 years at Princetown

until his death in 1929. For a large part of the duration of his stay he was entrusted to be a shepherd on the open moor, a job that he fell in love with and refused to give up. On his release from his first term of imprisonment he begged to stay on in the same capacity but this was refused. So he went out, committed a crime, and was sentenced to return to his beloved post. At lambing time David was allowed to stay out on the moors tending to his flock. The dedication of the man to his task was so considerable that after he died it is said he still returned to the moor that he knew and loved so much. Many is the foggy night when the spectral shape of this spirit shepherd can be seen fleeting amongst the bleating sheep. His grey outline is a shy one that disappears within seconds of being seen by any human – it is for his sheep that he haunts his old territory.

Princetown is supposedly the highest town in England and the Plume of Feathers is the oldest building in the town. It was built in 1785, many years before the prison. Not surprisingly such a wonderful old building has had its moments. The original ladies' loo, on the eastern side of the building, has been known to cause a few scares. On many occasions a sudden icy presence was felt and the effect was so scary that some ladies ran out with their undies down around their knees! No historical reason is known for this. Meanwhile, in a middle room upstairs, several guests complained that, whilst they have slumbered in their beds, they have had to hold onto their sheets whilst some invisible force tried to tug them off. Perhaps the ghost responsible for these mild indiscretions is a naughty one!

It is believed that long ago the sound of a mother sobbing was a frequent occurrence, her plight being the death of her child.

The landlord, the ever cheerful and charming James Langton, does not believe in ghosts but admitted that one night, whilst asleep in the top floor room, he was awoken by the unmistakable sounds of footsteps, which walked right across the bedroom and back again. The resident Labrador dogs would not go near this room, perhaps aware of an unnatural presence?

Since the building was re-roofed in 1983 none of these particular experiences have recurred but early one morning a lady, dressed in a brown cloak, walked the entire length of the inn. On inspection nobody could be found there which is strange because there are no exits and the building is solidly constructed. The witness of this was not immediately afraid of the passing person because she looked so real but, on realization of what had happened, was shaken for several days after the event.

Another obvious venue in Princetown is the cemetery where many French and American Prisoners of War are buried. They endured harsh and extreme conditions at Princetown and the number of untimely deaths has led to many sightings of ghosts at this spot.

Although there was a gap of almost forty years between the War Depot closing and the convict prison opening at Princetown, the two completely separate establishments are linked by one unusual ghost story.

An old lag serving a sentence for deception had managed to convince the authorities that he could be trusted to work outside the prison. But temptation overcame him and one misty day when nobody was looking, he slipped away from his working party.

Within hours he began to regret the folly of his actions because the Dartmoor mist made him lose his sense of direction. Ill-equipped for such a foolish venture, the old con lost his confidence and began to despair.

Suddenly, out of the mist loomed two marching figures dressed in early nineteenth century uniforms. Not stopping to question the two soldiers' presence on the moor, the convict hurriedly set off after them. In total silence they marched through the gloom until they walked straight into the lights of the search party out looking for him. But seconds before the recapture, the two accompanying troops suddenly vanished into thin air.

It is believed that these two men, from more than a century earlier, were part of a trio who perished on the moor in a blizzard. It has been calculated that the spot where the convict encountered them was probably the spot where two of them died. If you are ever out on the moor, make sure you have a map and compass, it's far more reliable than waiting to be rescued by a ghost!

*The main street at Princetown*

## Legions of Ghosts

Although the Romans paid little attention to Dartmoor, it is rumoured that the ancient camp on Hunter's Tor, above Lustleigh Cleave, was of Roman origin. This notion has been created because, when the moon is full, Roman legionnaires have been seen at this

Dark and Dastardly Dartmoor

spot. It seems that their spirits are condemned to fight a never-ending battle.

The Cleave is one of the loveliest, most wooded valleys on the moor. But take care if you happen to hear the sound of the hunt – it may not be quite what you think but another ghostly gathering. This hunting party is centuries old and has been seen by some locals riding through the valley dressed in Tudor garments. However, there have also been many other occasions when they have been heard without being seen – but in this case we wonder how it is known that this is the Tudor pack?

## Chagford's Cavalier Ghost

Sidney Godolphin, a young Cavalier, was mortally wounded by a musket shot, which hit him a little above his knee whilst he was in the porch of what is now The Three Crowns Hotel in Chagford. But the story does not quite end there because visitors staying at the inn have seen the figure of a Cavalier in the hotel corridors. The figure walks along a landing and just keeps going. One visitor actually identified him as Sidney, after a sighting, from a painting hanging in the hotel.

The Teign, above Chagford, has a delightful tributary called The Blackaton Brook. On one of the small stone bridges that spans the stream in the vicinity of Gidleigh, the sound of hand to hand fighting between Cavaliers and Roundheads has been frequently heard during the night.

## Castles in the Air?

Chagford, the ancient Stannary Town on the north eastern side of Dartmoor, has long been a favoured inland resort. For two Edwardian ladies from the smoke of London it was the ideal place to spend a holiday in the country. The ladies were so intent on having a wonderful time that they travelled down to Dartmoor for a brief stay to seek out the perfect place to rent.

Leaving their Chagford hotel, they went for a stroll to find their dream cottage and on the outskirts of the town they found it; a beautiful cottage garlanded in roses with neat lawns. Hoping, perhaps even presuming, that the cottage could be leased they knocked at the door, whereupon a pretty little girl dressed immaculately in white invited them into a lovely, neat sitting room. The girl's mother was also dressed in white and was beautifully ornamented with expensive jewellery. A cat lay contentedly asleep on a hearth rug and yes, it too was completely white.

The visiting ladies felt slightly uncomfortable but enquired whether they could rent the cottage. The dates they wanted were not available but they were so taken with the cottage that they agreed to change the date of their holiday so that they could have it. Arrangements made, they cheerfully returned to London.

However, when the ladies came back down to Devon they had the shock of their lives – for the cottage of their dreams had turned into a nightmare. Faced with a bed of nettles strewn with rubble it was clear that the cottage had been demolished many years before!

## The Ghost Bride of Chagford

At Chagford church lies Mary Whiddon who, in October 1641, walked up the aisle on her wedding day only to be cruelly shot down by a former lover. It was this sorry tale which R.D. Blackmore adapted into his famous story of *Lorna Doone*, cleverly disguised by a change of moor from Dartmoor to Exmoor.

Her family estate was Whiddon Park just over a mile from Chagford. In 1971 a daughter of the same house also got married at Chagford Church. One of the guests staying there for the event awoke at dawn to see the outline of a young bride dressed in a wedding dress, appropriate for the time when Mary Whiddon was shot. The modern bride placed her bouquet on Mary's grave, a gesture of respect, care and consideration for a troubled and wronged spirit.

## A Pack of Ghosts?

About three miles from here is an old manor farm house called Wonson. William Northmore, MP for Okehampton from 1713 to 1734 was a great gambler (or a terrible one) who lost a fortune on the turn of an ace of diamonds. To remind him of his own foolishness, he had an enormous six foot by six foot ace of diamonds painted onto one of the panels of the wainscot of his bedroom. Each night, on retiring to bed he would curse it, and the incident had such a profound effect on him he never touched another card again!

Now it is just possible that his ill fortune may have had a spiritual influence. It is believed that, if the door of the room is opened very carefully and quietly, four men dressed as cavaliers may be witnessed playing cards there! Fortunately the present occupants have not experienced this manifestation nor have they seen the friendly white lady ghost who has been known to tuck people into bed.

## Landlocked Sailors

Nearby is the Northmore Arms, one of the loveliest little pubs on the moor. Despite being as far from the sea as almost anyone could get in Devon, its ghost is that of an old bearded and bewhiskered sailor. He stands in the corner of the bar and has been seen by some of the locals and not necessarily after they have been drinking! Interestingly the pub lies on an ancient route that ran from parts of North Devon (Bideford and Barnstaple) down to Dartmouth and was called The Mariners' Way. This old mariner or sailor must have had cause to visit this wayside inn. The route was well used by sailors changing ship – it saved having to sail all around Cornwall and if you are so disposed you can even follow lengthy sections of the route yourself.

## Anyone Home?

There is a maze of lanes between Bovey Tracey and Haytor, the sort of rural area that looks as if nothing ever happens to it. The millions of visitors that pass close by on their way to Dartmoor never give it a second look but perhaps they should... At various times, from early this century until even quite recently, a strange phenomenon occurs. There have been several independent sightings, usually from people walking in the area, of a cottage seen below on the lower hillsides, beside a wood on a narrow, rough track. The strange thing is that no such cottage exists and people looking to locate it have been confounded by its non existence. Old maps confirm that no such cottage was ever there but the hedge, in the vicinity, contains myrtle, which was a favoured hedging plant by country folk and suggests that there might well have been a cottage here once. To live in a phantom cottage like this would certainly deal with unwanted callers or the postman delivering bills!

## The 9.15 pm Ghosts

There is a fine line between a cottage that may be described as quaint and one that is about to fall down. Millbrook Cottage at Moretonhampstead turned from the former into the latter for the Milton family who lived there during the Second World War so they moved out before it fell down around their ears. Behind them they left long rambling gardens, which were used by a local man in which to keep poultry. Now, although midnight is generally accepted as the 'witching hour' for 'ghoulies and ghosties and long legged beasties and things that go bump in the night', a series of ghostly occurrences happened at this derelict cottage at precisely 9.15 pm. The apparitions on each occasion were all different. A silhouetted figure seen against a moonlit snow scene left no footprints and vanished into thin air. Another man visiting the cottage, at 9.15 pm, was grabbed by the throat by an invisible force before being dumped unceremoniously on the ground. A small boy apparently ran through an open doorway but, as the church clock of Moreton struck 9.15 pm, the boy disappeared. There were many other disquieting events, which all coincided with this mid evening maelstrom of mysterious manifestations.

## The Golden Ghost

Dartmoor and the surrounding lands have always been difficult to farm and this was the case for the Collins family in the 1830s. Mary Collins laboured long and hard and managed to eke out an existence. But she could only work by day; every night she had to lock all the windows and bolt all the doors in order to keep out the forbidding figure of a tall ghost who stalked the farmyard and its outbuildings.

However, one night her son had a fever and cried out for water, but the water was outside in a courtyard well. Bravely Mary picked up a bright lantern and set off on her mission of mercy. As she drew the water from the well the tall ghost appeared beside her and challenged her presence in a deep bass voice, to which Mary replied, 'In the name of God why do you trouble me?' The ghost was so pleased that Mary had mentioned God in her response to him that he gently led her to a location on the farm where he told her that she must dig in the ground at first light. This she did and she came upon a crock of

gold coins,
which kept her and her
family in relative comfort for the rest
of their lives. The ghost was never seen again.

## Jay's Grave

Kitty Jay's wayside grave is sited on the road between Hound Tor and Heatree Cross. Solid facts are hard to establish about this young girl who is believed to have committed suicide after becoming pregnant out of wedlock. In keeping with tradition she had to be buried at the nearest crossroads rather than in the consecrated ground of a parish church cemetery. Until 1823 the law required that suicides and criminals should be buried at a crossroads with a stake through their bodies. The idea was that their troubled spirits would not be able to find their way back to the village.

Who Kitty Jay really was is not known for the story passed down through time has warped and distorted, although the 'bare bones' of the story are probably close to the truth. In 1860, James Bryant, a road mender, discovered bones in a rough grave and it was at first supposed they were that of an animal. When it was discovered they were from a young woman, his wife vaguely remembered a story told her by her own mother about an orphan girl who hanged herself. The bones were re-buried in their present position and for many years fresh flowers appeared daily on her grave, creating their own mystery as nobody knew who did this caring deed. It has been suggested by some that it is the pixies who leave them, others say that Beatrice Chase, the eccentric novelist who discovered the sad story of a Mary Jay who hanged herself, was responsible. It is now most likely that her story has been told so often that people consider it a sign of good luck to leave a small posy of moorland flowers on her grave.

Her ghost has reputedly been seen hovering over the grave by people travelling past, although this is unsubstantiated but even so some folk will go on quite lengthy detours to avoid the spot.

There are other suicide victims buried in similar circumstances at different locations on Dartmoor, the most notable being George Stephens whose grave is on the high, open moor, a few miles from Peter Tavy. But as no-one has ever created a mystery over his name, his death or fresh flowers appearing on his grave, he only merits a brief mention here!

## Tom White and the Pixies

Dartmoor wouldn't be Dartmoor without its pixies, those mischievous little creatures who so densely populate the moor. Stories abound but we only have room here for one short one.

There once lived a handsome young moor man called Tom White. He was fit and strong and thought nothing of walking four miles (we don't think much of it either!) across Bellever Tor and down to Huccaby Farm on the West Dart River to meet his sweetheart.

One night Tom left Huccaby and started home. Beyond Laughter Tor he dropped to the East Dart River where he heard music nearby. Then he saw hundreds of tiny pixies having their own discotheque, dancing and prancing and jumping about. Naturally Tom was spotted and he was forced to dance with them and, although he became weary, he simply could not stop until dawn. The pixies disappeared leaving Tom in a state of complete exhaustion. He vowed never to go out on the moor at night again – a promise so seriously taken that he forsook his young lady at Huccaby. Well, that was his story anyway!

## Vixana the Witch

An appropriate story to end this little look at the dark and dastardly deeds of deepest Dartmoor is with Vixana, the ugliest old crone of a witch ever to darken the moors. The legendary Vixana had a face as wrinkled as a walnut, liberally spiced with a profusion of warts and spots. Her hair was like straggly straw, her teeth were green, black and festering and her nose was long and hooked. She was as evil as she was ugly and this diabolical person made her home from a rockpile close to a major path across the moor on the Two Bridges to Tavistock Road. Beside it was a mire, so deep it would easily accommodate all who stepped in it – not always by accident!

Whenever a wayfarer passed close to her home she would use her evil powers to conjure up a mist. Totally lost the poor victim would eventually wander into the mire and be drawn into a vat of mud and ooze whilst the wicked witch stood and gloated.

Well, of course the moor folk were not over enthusiastic about such goings on and were desperately keen to rid the moor of such an evil force. By a sheer stroke of good luck there just happened to be a handsome young moor man who had been awarded a magic ring as a result of services rendered to the pixies. Whenever he put this ring on he became invisible.

And so the moor man was employed to sort out the evil Vixana. As he approached her tor she spied him and immediately conjured up a mist, which completely enshrouded him. But he kept his wits about him and put on his magic ring. He cleverly avoided the dire mire to reach the base of the tor, one of the highest granite piles on the moor. With his great strength and sure-footedness he stealthily and silently climbed to the top of the tor where the perplexed witch stood peering into the mist. As she dwelled on where the young man had gone, he rushed towards her and threw her over the cliff face where, with no time to grab her broomstick, she crashed to a spectacular death. The End!